Disclaimer

This book has been written for information purposes only. Every effort has been made to make this book as complete and accurate as possible.

However, there may be mistakes in typography or content. Also, this book provides information only up to the publishing date. Therefore, this book should be used as a guide - not as the ultimate source.
The purpose of this book is to educate. Neither the author nor the publisher warrant that the information contained in this book is fully complete and shall not be responsible for any errors or omissions.

The author and publisher shall have neither liability nor responsibility to any person or entity with respect to any loss or damage caused or alleged to be caused directly or indirectly by this book.

This book is neither designed nor intended to offer legal or financial advice. Please seek appropriate legal and financial counsel.

Dedication

This book is dedicated to my grandparents, Wesley and Annie. I couldn't have been any luckier. I miss you all! #RIP

To my parents, Michael and Sharon. Thank you for all the guidance. The first 40 years were the hardest! Dinner on me!

To my brother, Malcolm. Thanks for the encouragement that you give unknowingly.

To my kids, Miriam (Mimi), WJ and Brandon. I hope this book serves as a reminder to you all throughout the coming years that you really can do anything you put your mind to! #ROLLCALL #OWENS

To all my friends who have become family over the years. Thank you for all the love, support and lessons that turned into blessings.

- Love and Light...Wesley B. Owens

Foreword

Imagine purchasing and reading a book that taught you how to make thousands, if not millions, by investing in real estate. Is that possible? Yes, and this is just the book to teach you. Real estate is one of the foundations for building wealth and learning about this proven and trusted industry should be a priority. I have been involved in the real estate industry for over 23 years and I continue to learn something new on a regular basis. Over my career, I have been involved in over 1000 transactions including wholesaling, fixing/flipping, multifamily, single family, commercial, land, etc. In 2015, my team and I launched a program/course called Flipology 101: The Boot Camp. This program was designed to teach investors of every experience level how to successfully flip houses in any area. This course provides the resources necessary to be successful and we are always vetting more resources so that we provide you with the best. Since 2015, we have trained 1000s of people from all over the world.

I am very passionate about the real estate industry and helping others build wealth, which is why I will continue to teach, help and support anyone that wants to learn about and invest in real estate. Funny thing is on a daily basis, people call, text, or contact me in some way asking if they can "PICK MY BRAIN". I do my best to allow as many people as possible to do so, but I honestly just don't have the time. It's amazing how God works! When my good friend, Wesley, called me and told me about his book, I was so excited for several reasons. One, my good friend was writing a book on a topic that I love. Two, he was creating another resource to help the world. Three, it gave us time to talk about ways to provide better resources in the industry.

Go Ahead...Pick My Brain: A Comprehensive Guide to Investing in Real Estate

I have known Wesley for over 2 decades now and have watched him grow tremendously and help other people grow as well. He is one of the most intelligent people I know and I truly respect his business acumen. Hence, why I am excited about this amazing book. He is encouraging EVERYONE to PICK HIS BRAIN! Isn't that great? This book is going to teach you the processes, strategies, and resources to be successful in this business.

I want to congratulate you for making the decision to read this book and for deciding to enter into a positively life changing industry. I want to thank Wesley for making this book happen. I wish you much success on your journey to building wealth!

- Ramon Tookes, JD

Table of Contents

Introductory

A lot of people these days are preaching about the buy and hold method of gaining wealth with real estate.

There indeed may come a time in your life or business when you'll want to hang onto a piece of property, most likely you'll only be interested in keeping certain types of property. If you're just starting out, flipping a house may be an ideal way to get started.

Basically, there are three ways that you can flip a house, although each one has its own terms, motivation, and house type. The first method is known as retailing. Retailing is when you buy a house in bad shape, do the repairs to fix it up, then turn around and sell it at market value.

There are a variety of houses in need of repairs out there, and several ways that you can quickly flip a house to net profit. All you need to know are the techniques that will get you the most money in the least amount of time.

The second way you can flip a house is through wholesaling. Wholesaling involves finding a

Go Ahead...Pick My Brain: A Comprehensive Guide to Investing in Real Estate

home for sale then flipping it to an investor for a fast, yet small profit.

To do this, you'll need to know the real estate investors in your area, the types of homes that flip the best, and how to fund your property so you can flip it to them in a timely fashion. If you live in a major city, you'll find that using the wholesaling method of flipping houses is actually easier to accomplish.

The third way to flip a house is by assigning the purchase contract. Using this method, you'll commit to buy the house from the seller. But, instead of closing the deal yourself, you'll assign the contract to a real estate investor - of course for a small fee. The investor will take the contract over and close the purchase themselves - flipping the house.

This can be very profitable, especially if you invest in the right home. You don't need to have your contract worded any special way, although you will need to determine an appropriate assignment fee.

If you're looking to break into the real estate market and make big bucks, you'll need to learn all about flipping houses. Flipping houses is very profitable, especially once you have learned the basics. The first and third methods

Go Ahead...Pick My Brain: A Comprehensive Guide to Investing in Real Estate

are the best, although they will both take quite a bit of work on your part.

Restoring homes isn't easy, and you'll need to have a team qualified to handle any repairs. Assigning the purchase may be difficult when you first start out, although it will get easier with time. If you stay at it and do your best to make a profit - you'll be an expert at flipping homes in no time at all.

Go Ahead...Pick My Brain: A Comprehensive Guide to Investing in Real Estate

Chapter 1: Flipping Houses for Fast Real Estate Profit

People will laugh at your dreams, then hate you when you make them come true.

One of the rising stars when it comes to real estate investment is known as 'flipping' properties. This works by buying properties that are in need of either minor cosmetic repairs or in need of serious renovations, doing the work, and selling the home for a much greater price. In theory, this brings in a significant amount of profit in a rather small amount of time. Hence, the word "fast".

This is the case for many who attempt to flip properties, but it takes a little more than the idea in order to make the process work. For this reason, there are many who end up sacrificing profit or losing money in the process when plans aren't well conceived.

If you are considering a future in real estate investing, this is one of the quickest ways in which investors can turn a profit. Even more so, it is a method for bringing in high profit in a short amount of time. Unfortunately, this once closely guarded secret has gained some degree of infamy and there is fierce competition for the undervalued properties on the market as more and more would be investors decide to throw their hats into the collective ring.

If you are considering real estate investments in general and house flipping in particular there are a couple of things you should keep in mind:

1. Treat this as a business rather than a hobby. Far too many investors do not take their investments seriously. This is a mistake because in this business time is money and every month that the house isn't sold is a month that the house is costing you money. Create a plan, make a schedule, and stick to them both.

2. Remember, this is a business. You are not investing in properties to make friends or seem nice. You are in this business to turn a profit. You cannot be timid about making lower than market offers. The ability to buy low and sell high is the lifeblood of this business. To that end, you are quite likely going to hurt feelings and make people angry (because they often price their homes

Go Ahead...Pick My Brain: A Comprehensive Guide to Investing in Real Estate

with emotion. Many times these prices are simply not feasible economically). If you cannot deal with this reality, then you are going to have some degree of difficulty gaining the high profits you are seeking. In this business nice guys finish last. And, while you can be kind in your business dealings you can't afford to let emotions stop you from making a fair profit in this line of work.

3. Pay attention to the market. This is vitally important. Many 'flippers' lost their shirts in the 2008 collapse of the housing market around the U.S. The truth of the matter is that the indicators had been building for years. In cities where there was once a shortage of viable housing options there were suddenly surpluses.

Now, you need to understand, this does not drive the value of properties down so much as it brings them back to their proper values. Investors that were counting on an ability to sell above the actual value of the property were left holding the bag on these properties for quite some time until they could be sold. Some never managed to sell these properties and were left dealing with the debt service in addition to the costs of the upgrades.

Go Ahead...Pick My Brain: A Comprehensive Guide to Investing in Real Estate

*TIP Do not buy in an inflated market if it can be avoided unless it is during the very beginning of the inflation (before property developers can create a surplus).

4. Do not allow it to become personal. Far too many first-time house flippers decide to create a work of art rather than a business investment. It is tempting when making cosmetic and structural repairs to go ahead and create a dream home.

The problem with this is that depending on the particular market you are unlikely to recoup the costs involved in doing so. The goal is to invest little and profit large. Granite countertops are lovely but not at all necessary in a neighborhood filled with those of humble means. Cater to the tastes and budgets of your target market rather than your personal tastes.

Despite the risks involved in flipping houses as a real estate investment there is no denying that fortunes have been made doing just that. Even in the current housing market there is a great deal of promise available to those who can do the work quickly and inexpensively. People still want to buy these lovely homes rather than buying a home that needs to be made over after the price of purchasing.

Chapter 2: Flipping Houses for Fun and Profit

The best way to get on your feet is to get off your ass!

For those of you who watch on the edge of your seats week after week as people on television seek to successfully turn a lump of coal into a diamond that is suitable for kings and queens to call home, it is quite possible that you have considered 'flipping' a home of your own.

This is a great way to make a nice tidy profit in real estate rather quickly if proper planning and attention to detail is made in the process.

Believe it or not, when done correctly and within reasonable time and budget constraints, projects such as this can be a great challenge and a ton of fun. First of all, the average citizen isn't allowed to play with power tools on a regular basis and Tim Allen has taught us exactly how fun power tools can be.

Keep in mind that he has also taught us just how dangerous they can be as well. The point is that it is often fun to learn new things and

Go Ahead...Pick My Brain: A Comprehensive Guide to Investing in Real Estate

for many of us, working with power tools is a new thing. For those experienced with power tools, there are still likely to be some fun new things on the horizon when doing a real estate flip.

Even if power tools aren't exactly your cup of tea, perhaps you have always wanted to try your hand at creating a color scheme or a trial run at renovating a kitchen or bathroom. Beyond a great way to have fun while turning a profit, a house flip can be a great practice session for changes you'd like to make within your own home.

Most of us learn best by making mistakes. Isn't it best to make mistakes with Formica® or Corian® rather than the granite countertops we'd prefer in our own kitchens and baths?

This also gives you the opportunity to see how things you are considering for your home look in other homes before incorporating them into your home. If you are considering a certain type of laminate flooring, try it in a house that you are flipping. This is the ultimate opportunity to use trial and error when making design and décor plans for your own home. Even better is the fact that you can work towards a profit as you do just that and I personally do not know of anyone that does

Go Ahead...Pick My Brain: A Comprehensive Guide to Investing in Real Estate

not appreciate a nice hefty bit of profit every now and then.

Another fun thing about flipping real estate is that you often get the opportunity to work with the people you love. This is a great opportunity to get friends and family involved in the process of creating a masterpiece right by your side.

The price for their time and labor is often some good music, a tasty pizza, and a couple of cold sodas (or beers provided the work is done for the day and everyone is walking home of course).

Even children can be of some help in these projects though you want to be very careful that they aren't too much help with power tools and paintbrushes. Typically have older children help with landscaping projects and find someone to care for younger children (the tools, fumes, and temptations for small children simply may prove too risky to be practical).

*TIP Attend the home improvement classes at a national home improvement retailer near you. The classes are often free of charge and you will get to test drive the power tools while learning some new techniques.

Go Ahead...Pick My Brain: A Comprehensive Guide to Investing in Real Estate

Chapter 3: Benefits of Flipping Real Estate

The hardest walk you can make is the walk you make alone. But that is the walk that makes you the strongest.

The obvious benefit and sought-after benefit of flipping real estate is the profit. This is one incredibly tangible benefit, particularly when the profits are large and quick to come your way. Of course, there are risks. Most ventures that offer high profit also come with a high degree of risk. Money, however, is not the only benefit that can be associated with flipping real estate though it is certainly the one on most investors' minds when they get into this line of work.

Let's talk profit first. Profit is the one reason that most people get into this business. The days are long and the work is hard. This is definitely not the type of work one would ordinarily undertake for the simple love of getting one's hands dirty.

This is real work that leaves you bone weary at the end of the day. However, when all the

Go Ahead...Pick My Brain: A Comprehensive Guide to Investing in Real Estate

work is done and you get around to making the sell, you will find that the profit involved in a successful flip is well worth the effort you've put into the process.

The good news is that the savvy investor can still manage to make money even when the situation may not work out quite as planned. This is yet another benefit to flipping real estate. If the flip doesn't work out, there is always the option of leasing to own the property or renting the property out.

The profits in these situations are considerably less than a straight out flip but it can prevent financial ruin that is often the risk of a flip gone wrong. The fact that there are options and that you aren't necessarily left ruined at the end of a bad flip is a benefit. There aren't many types of investments that allow you the option to save yourself the way real estate does.

One of the intangible benefits of flipping houses is that you are working for yourself. In other words, you do not have to punch a time clock or worry about overtime (at least not on your part). This can be a bad thing too if you lack the discipline required to get the job done. However, most of us will view this as a huge check in the pros column when deciding

Go Ahead...Pick My Brain: A Comprehensive Guide to Investing in Real Estate

whether to take the plunge into the wonderful and frightening world of real estate investing.

Even though this is a business that requires a lot of work in order to turn an attractive profit there is some satisfaction at the end of the day involved in knowing that you are working for yourself and not to make someone else wealthy or in order to punch a time clock.

That feeling of satisfaction is one that you should hang onto when the brand-new toilet you've just installed becomes a geyser. Of course, there are mistakes along the way, what other job keeps you on your toes quite like this one?

Real estate investing, house flipping, can be one of the most frustrating types of investments a soul can pursue. At the same time, it can also be one of the most rewarding mentally, spiritually, and financially. This is something you should keep in mind when deciding whether this is the right path for you.

Go Ahead...Pick My Brain: A Comprehensive Guide to Investing in Real Estate

Chapter 4: Choosing Your Real Estate Appraiser

The only fence against the world is the thorough knowledge of it. (John Locke)

If you have been thinking about purchasing a real estate property for personal use or as an investment, you'll need to hire the services of a real estate appraiser.

If you plan to finance your home through a bank or hard money lender, you'll more than likely need to get the property appraised first. Banks and most lenders want to know the value of the home for your protection, as well as make sure that the home they are financing is worth the total amount that you take on the loan.

In most cases, the appraisal indicates that the home does indeed meet or exceed the asking price. In some cases, however, the appraisal will come back saying that the home is worth less than the selling price. If this is the case, the buyer normally must either drop the deal or try to negotiate with the seller to get a price that meets the appraisal.

For those very reasons, a real estate appraiser is very important. When you are dealing with a home, one appraisal can make a deal or break it. Even if you are not financing your purchase through a hard money lender or the bank, you should still try to get the home appraised and find out the true value.

You should also make a point to find the best appraiser that you can afford. If you hire an appraiser who isn't that experienced, you'll pay for it later when you discover that the property isn't worth what you paid for it.

A real estate appraiser will go through the home performing an evaluation, and then provide you with a written evaluation after he has gathered all necessary information. Appraisers will also take into consideration the replacement costs as well. Also, they will have to verify legal descriptions as well. There is a lot of work involved with appraisals, which is why it's so very important that each step of the process is performed correctly by a licensed, qualified real estate appraiser.

If you have a real estate agent, he or she will more than likely be able to make a recommendation. Keep in mind that this doesn't mean the recommendation is the best; it's just someone who your agent works with.

To ensure that you get the right appraisal on your home you'll need to find yourself an appraiser who can complete the job.

When you look for your real estate appraiser, you should look for someone who comes highly recommended. You can ask family and friends for their opinions, or search local papers, even the Internet. If you take your time and search for the best real estate appraiser that you can find – you'll normally get an appraisal that is right on target.

Go Ahead...Pick My Brain: A Comprehensive Guide to Investing in Real Estate

Chapter 5: Things to Avoid When Flipping Real Estate

Those too lazy to plow in the right season will have no food at the harvest.

Flipping property is rising in popularity as a form of real estate investing. The truth of the matter is that this is one of the more entertaining methods for many investors that are simply 'itching' to get their hands a little dirty.

The sweat equity involved in these transactions, while attractive, can also be daunting when skills are inadequate and out and out dangerous in some situations.

If you are one of the many around the world who consider the appeal of flipping property with huge dollar signs in your eyes, you should take care to avoid the following things in order to minimize your risks while maximizing your potential for success.

1. Do **not** fail to have a qualified inspection of the property before any money changes hands. If you do not have any idea of the types of work that needs to be done, then you cannot possibly make an educated estimate of the costs involved in rehabbing the property.

2. Do not underestimate the budget for repairs on the flip. This is one of the most common mistakes that even seasoned professionals make, and it can mean the difference between a profit and a loss on the property if you aren't careful and do not stick to the planned budget.

3. Do not overestimate your abilities. This is another common mistake. The fact that you've seen something done on television doesn't mean that it is something you can do on your own. It costs more money and time to have someone come in and repair your mistakes than to have had a professional do the work from the beginning.

This doesn't mean that you can't learn how to do some of the work or that doing so wouldn't be cost effective. The trick lies in determining where your skills and abilities can really take

Go Ahead...Pick My Brain: A Comprehensive Guide to Investing in Real Estate

you rather than where you hope they will take you. Plumbing, electrical, and structural work are generally best left to the professionals unless you have specific experience or training in these fields.

4. Do **not** fail to hold yourself accountable to your timetable and your budget. Real estate investing puts you in the boss's seat and while that is often simple when it comes to driving others, we often have a bit of difficulty when it comes to holding ourselves accountable for time and money along the way. Unfortunately, failing to do so can be a very costly blunder.

5. Do **not** forget to keep up with receipts, bills, etc. and reconcile the facts and figures daily. It is far too simple to allow a couple of trips to the local home improvement center escape careful scrutiny.

Add a couple of these trips per day and you could easily find thousands of dollars missing from your budget with no paper trail to explain the transactions. You could also find that some tools will not work or be needed for the project. Those items cannot typically be returned without the original receipts.

6. Avoid having too many "chiefs" on the project. If this is your ball game, then you need to run with it rather than having 10 people giving contradictory orders. Schedule meetings regularly with contractors to discuss progress and any adjustments or changes that may need to be made.

7. Avoid poor planning. This is one step that is the difference between success and failure for many would-be house flippers. Plan out every step of the project in an order that makes sense. You do not want to paint the ceilings or walls after you've installed new floors. Nor do you want to rip out walls in order to replace plumbing after you've painted them.

Plan things out in the proper order and allow a day or two between subsequent projects in case extra time is needed. The last thing you want to do is pay a group of contractors to stand around waiting for the paint to dry so they can begin the next step in the process.

There are risks involved in any type of investment. While real estate is one of the

Go Ahead...Pick My Brain: A Comprehensive Guide to Investing in Real Estate

greatest things in the world in which people can invest, there are still risks.

Following the advice above, however can significantly lower those risks and give investors the opportunity to have great expectations when all is said and done. Whether this will be your first flip or your fortieth flip there is much that can be reviewed in the steps above that will reaffirm many of the things you've learned along the way.

Chapter 6: Tips for Selling Your Property

One small positive thought can change your whole day.

Unlike other things that you may own, you can never take selling your property lightly. An investment property is a big commodity, one that is worth a lot of money. Before you even think about selling your property, you should put a lot of thought and consideration into it. Although you may want to sell your property - you should make sure that you do it the right way.

The first thing you should do when you are thinking of selling your property is to hire yourself a qualified real estate agent who knows the neighborhood. An agent who knows the neighborhood will know the ideal price for your property, and help you sell it at the ideal price.

If your property is priced right for the neighborhood, chances are it will sell. If it is priced too high, you might not get any offers, or anyone interested in buying the property.

Go Ahead...Pick My Brain: A Comprehensive Guide to Investing in Real Estate

Once you have a real estate agent, you and your agent will need to develop a strategy. You'll need to decide on the price and how long you will leave it on the market before you think about a reduction.

You'll also need to discuss his commission as well, which will help to avoid any misunderstandings in the future. If you talk about these types of things when you first start out selling your property, you'll find the entire process to go much smoother.

In some cases, you may run out of time before you are able to sell your property. In this situation, you may want to rent out your property. When you rent out your property, you may also be able to strike a deal with renters that your property is available for showing. To make the house accessible to potential buyers, you may want to offer your renters a lower price. This way, they will be more inclined to make the house available for potential buyers.

Keep in mind that selling your property will take you some time. You can also sell it yourself if you prefer, without a real estate agent. This can save you quite a bit of money as well, as you won't have to pay a real estate agent.

If you are planning to go this route, you should make sure that you know the value of your property and you know the neighborhood. You can put a "for sale by owner" sign in the yard, and list your property in local newspapers, and on the Internet as well.

This way, you'll get your property out to the market of potential buyers. Properties that are for sale by the owner are always great for buyers - as they can deal with the owner directly and not have to worry about dealing with any real estate agents.

Go Ahead...Pick My Brain: A Comprehensive Guide to Investing in Real Estate

Chapter 7: Determine the Listing Price

Not seeing results? Feel like giving up? Consider this: the LAST thing to grow on a fruit tree is the fruit.

When it comes to buying a home, most potential buyers will use the listing price as the number one factor to determine the homes that they look at.

Even though you and a realtor may determine the listing price, the buyer will determine the selling price. If the price is too high, most buyers won't give it a second thought - which is why you want to determine the listing price carefully.

If you set the correct price, you'll notice a much faster sale. Setting the right listing price will also attract more potential buyers to your property as well. You'll also notice an increase in response from realtors and receive more calls about the property. The listing price is very important - and it can ultimately determine whether you sale your property.

A home can be overpriced due to several reasons. Overpricing is something you want to avoid, as buyers tend to steer clear of homes that have been overpriced. Normally, this happens when a buyer asks a lot more than the home is worth or valued at.

Some buyers ask a lot more than the value of the home due to location. Although the location is very important, most potential buyers won't give the home a second look if they think the price is too high - and more importantly out of their price range.

When you put your home up for sale, most activity will happen within the first couple of weeks. If you put the right price on your home, you'll notice immediate interest. There are always buyers looking for homes in their price range, waiting for new homes to be listed or homes to be reduced in price. Buyers who are waiting to purchase may miss seeing your home completely if the price is too high.

To determine the listing price of your home, you should always have it appraised before you put it on the market. This way, you'll know the full value of your home. You can sell it for market value or go a little under, although you should never attempt to go way over the value. In doing so, you'll miss out on a lot of potential buyers. The home market is very competitive these days, which is why you want your home to draw as much interest as possible.

Keep in mind that realtors really have no control at all over the real estate market, only the plan behind marketing. Realtors don't determine the asking price - the seller does. You can ask a realtor for advice, although you are the decider of your listing price. If you do things right and take each thing step by step, you'll set the listing price in the right area and have no problems selling your property.

*TIP Engage a realtor to do a market survey BEFORE you buy an investment property to determine what price comparable properties are selling for before you buy.

Go Ahead...Pick My Brain: A Comprehensive Guide to Investing in Real Estate

Chapter 8: Common Risks Faced by Property Flippers

Work harder than you think you did yesterday.

The first thing that should be noted is that flipping houses is a great way to bring home a rather large profit in a relatively short amount of time when doing so in a seller's market so to speak.

The problem is that we currently seem to be experiencing what is known as a buyer's market from one end of the United States to another. Foreclosures are at an all-time high, which means that the market has suddenly been saturated with properties for sale.

While this is excellent news (believe it or not) when it comes to getting your hands on a property at a lower price, it also makes a difficult time of convincing buyers to pay top dollar when there are better bargains down the road.

This of course is one of the primary risks involved in the real estate investment venture that is known as flipping properties. The massive profits that most investors seek cannot be accomplished if the property cannot be purchased, rehabbed, and sold quickly.

Unfortunately, now, very few properties in any city are selling terribly quickly. The worst-case scenario in a situation like this is that you are forced to either absorb the loss (which can in extreme cases result in serious financial hardship or bankruptcy) or rent the property out (which will in most cases negate all the efforts that were made to rehab the property.

An inability to sell the property that is being flipped is probably the worst fear of every property investor who engages in this sort of investment. In these cases, it is often better to drop the price and take a loss than hold out for a better price risking further loss in the future.

These are not the only risks associated with flipping properties unfortunately. Another risk is seriously underestimating the amount of money that will be required in order to do the necessary work.

This is something that many first-time investors find is a common occurrence. Most

Go Ahead...Pick My Brain: A Comprehensive Guide to Investing in Real Estate

people have unrealistic expectations of exactly how far their dollars will go when it comes to investing in the materials and labor needed to properly rehab a property.

Even minor cosmetic repairs throughout a house can easily run into several thousands of dollars in order to repair. The flip side is that once these repairs are made the potential profits run into several tens of thousands of dollars.

Another risk that isn't often considered is the risk of overestimating abilities.
This is one risk that costs not only precious time but valuable money as well.

Not only is material wasted in the process of discovering you aren't exactly skilled in any particular tasks but also there are further expenses (often unplanned) involved in hiring the professional to repair the damage and replace the material that was wasted. When in doubt, it is almost always best to hire a professional if possible.

This also leads to missing deadlines, going seriously off schedule, and adding yet another mortgage payment (if not more than one) to the overall price of the project.

The final risk is often something that simply cannot be seen or anticipated. This was experienced in the days immediately following 9-11 and should not be forgotten. The unforeseen happens every day. Markets crash; local economies can be devastated by the announcement of a major employer that it is going out of business (think of the collapse of companies such as Enron and World Comm and what they did to local economies).

In these instances, the market will take quite a while to recover from the shock to its system and 'flippers' among other investors are often left feeling just as lost and devastated as those that were victimized by these companies-both through no fault of their own.

Stuff happens and those things that we have absolutely no control over are almost always the things that affect us most profoundly. The same holds true when it comes to property investment. The state of the economy, the housing market in an area, and sudden announcements that affect either can often have the most profound impact on those who are investing in property in those areas whether for better or for worse. The trick is in deciding which risks are acceptable.

Glossary:

1. Adjustable-rate mortgage

There are two types of conventional loans: the fixed-rate and the adjustable-rate mortgage. In an adjustable-rate mortgage, the interest rate can change over the course of the loan at five, seven, or ten-year intervals. For homeowners who plan to stay in their home for more than a few years, this is a risky loan as rates can suddenly skyrocket depending on market conditions.

2. Amortization

This is the process of combining both interest and principal in payments, rather than simply paying off interest at the start. This allows you to build more equity in the home early on.

3. Appraisal

In order to get a loan from a bank to buy a home, you first need to get the home appraised so the bank can be sure they are lending the correct amount of money. The appraiser will determine the value of the home based on an examination of the property itself, as well as the sale price of comparable homes in the area.

Go Ahead...Pick My Brain: A Comprehensive Guide to Investing in Real Estate

4. Assessed value

This is how much a home is worth according to a public tax assessor who makes that determination in order to figure out how much city or state tax the owner owes.

5. Buyer's agent

This is the agent who represents the buyer in the home-buying process. On the other side is the listing agent, who represents the seller.

6. Cash reserves

The cash reserves is the money left over for the buyer after the down payment and the closing costs.

7. Closing

The closing refers to the meeting that takes place where the sale of the property is finalized. At the closing, buyers and sellers sign the final documents, and the buyer makes the down payment and pays closing costs.

8. Closing costs

In addition to the final price of a home, there are also closing costs, which will typically make up about **two to five percent of the purchase price**, not including the down payment.

Go Ahead...Pick My Brain: A Comprehensive Guide to Investing in Real Estate

Examples of closings costs include loan processing costs, title insurance, and excise tax.

9. Comparative market analysis

Comparative market analysis (CMA) is a report on comparable homes in the area that is used to derive an accurate value for the home in question.

10. Contingencies

This term refers to conditions that must be met for the purchase of a home to be finalized. For example, there may be contingencies that the appraised value must be near the final sale price.

11. Dual agency

Dual agency is when one agent represents both sides, rather than having both a buyer's agent and a listing agent.

12. Equity

Equity is ownership. In homeownership, equity refers to how much of your home you own. The more equity you have, the more financial flexibility you have. Put another way, equity is the difference between the fair market value of the home and the unpaid balance of the

Go Ahead...Pick My Brain: A Comprehensive Guide to Investing in Real Estate

mortgage. If you have a $200,000 home, and you still owe $150,000 on it, you have $50,000 in equity.

13. Escrow

Escrow is an account that the lender sets up that receives monthly payments from the buyer.

14. Fixed-rate mortgage

There are two types of conventional loans: the fixed-rate and the adjustable-rate mortgage. In a fixed-rate mortgage, the interest rate stays the same throughout the life of the loan.

15. Home warranty

This warranty protects from future problems to things such as plumbing and heating, which can be extremely expensive to fix.

16. Inspection

Home inspections are required once a potential buyer makes an offer. Typically, they cost a few hundred dollars. The purpose is to check that the house's plumbing, foundation, appliances, and other features are up to code. Issues that may turn up during an inspection may factor into the negotiation on a final price. Failing to do an inspection may result in surprise costly repairs down the road for the home buyer.

17. Interest

This is the cost of borrowing money for a home. Interest is combined with principal to determine monthly mortgage payments. The longer a mortgage is, the more you will pay in interest when you have finally paid off the loan.

18. Listing

A listing is essentially a home that is for sale. The term gets its name from the fact that these homes are often "listed" on a website or in a publication.

19. Listing agent

This is the agent who represents the seller in the home-buying process. On the other side is the buyer's agent, who represents the buyer.

20. Mortgage broker

The broker is an individual or company that is responsible for taking care of all aspects of the deal between borrowers and lenders, whether that be originating the loan or placing it with a funding source such as a bank.

Go Ahead...Pick My Brain: A Comprehensive Guide to Investing in Real Estate

21. Offer

This is the initial price offered by a prospective buyer to the seller. A seller may accept the offer, reject it, or counter with a different offer.

22. Pre-approval letter

Before buying a home, a buyer can obtain a pre-approval letter from a bank, which provides an estimate on how much the bank will lend that person. This letter will help determine what the buyer can afford.

23. Principal

The principal is the amount of money borrowed to purchase a home. Paying off the principal allows a buyer to build equity in a home. Principal is combined with interest to determine the monthly mortgage payment.

24. Private mortgage insurance

Private mortgage insurance (PMI) is an insurance premium that the buyer pays to the lender in order to protect the lender from default on a mortgage. These insurance payments typically end once the buyer builds up 20% equity in a home.

Go Ahead...Pick My Brain: A Comprehensive Guide to Investing in Real Estate

25. Real estate agent

A real estate agent is a professional with a real estate license who works under a broker and assists both buyers and sellers in the home-buying process.

26. Real estate broker

A real estate broker is a real estate agent who has passed a state broker's exam and met a minimum number of transactions. These brokers are able to work on their own or hire their own agents.

27. Realtor

A Realtor is a real estate agent who specifically is a member of the National Association of Realtors. NAR has a code of standards and ethics that members must adhere to.

28. Refinancing

Refinancing is when you restructure your home loan, replacing your old loan with an entirely new loan that has different rates and payment structures. The main reason people refinance their home loans is to get a lower interest rate on their mortgage, and therefore lower not only the monthly payment but also the overall debt owed.

Go Ahead...Pick My Brain: A Comprehensive Guide to Investing in Real Estate

29. Title insurance

Title insurance is often required as part of the closing costs. It covers research into public records to ensure that the title is free and clear, and ready for sale. If you purchase a home and find out later that there are liens on the home, you'll be glad you had title insurance.

Bonus:
Finding Motivated Sellers

1. Tired landlords
2. List of eviction court attendants
3. Mailers to Out of state landlords
4. Mailers to Landlords who own more than one property with back taxes
5. Mailers to Landlords who own tax delinquent multi-family properties
6. Buy a "leads list" of landlords
7. Mailers to property owners whose assessment went way up this year
8. Mailers to properties that were owned by known investors who went out of business
9. Mailers to out of state landlords/owners of multifamily houses
10. Mailers to tax delinquent homeowners
11. Place "**We Buy Houses**" flyers/business cards at unemployment offices.
12. One-page flyers posted on bulletin boards at grocery stores.
13. Mailers to vacant land owners
14. Using Craigslist to find sellers:
15. Post ad that states, "**We Buy Houses**"
16. Send emails to craigslist ads with apartments for rent

Go Ahead...Pick My Brain: A Comprehensive Guide to Investing in Real Estate

17. Mailers to specific zip codes asking if they want to sell or know someone who does
18. Mailers to people getting divorced
19. Mailers to divorce attorneys who can refer clients to you
20. Mailers/emails to FSBOs
21. Send mailers to expired MLS listings
22. Post ad on www.Craigslist.org: We buy houses
23. Send mailers to properties purchased between 1k-50k within last five years (owner might be a want to-be flipper who did nothing with property)
24. Send mailers to estate Executors/Administrators
25. Send mailers to estate/probate attorneys (consider having your attorney send letter, business cards to estate attorneys because attorneys always open mail from other attorneys)
26. Bandit signs: **We Buy Houses**
27. Big baller marketing: TV, billboards, radio ads
28. Send mailers to out of state owners who have owned for more than x years
29. Send mailers to building code violators
30. Send mailers to health code violators
31. Send mailers to people facing foreclosure
32. Purchase leads lists of folks who inherited homes

Go Ahead...Pick My Brain: A Comprehensive Guide to Investing in Real Estate

Notes:

Go Ahead...Pick My Brain: A Comprehensive Guide to Investing in Real Estate

www.ingramcontent.com/pod-product-compliance
Lightning Source LLC
Chambersburg PA
CBHW021829190326
41518CB00007B/797